TED STUDEBAKER:
A Man Who Loved Peace

Story by Joy Hofacker Moore
Drawings by Jim Guenthner

HERALD PRESS
Scottdale, Pennsylvania
Kitchener, Ontario
1987

Library of Congress Cataloging-in-Publication Data

Moore, Joy Hofacker, 1952-
    Ted Studebaker : a man who loved peace.

Summary: Traces the life of a conscientious objector
who followed his religious beliefs in choosing not to
fight, volunteered to serve in Vietnam as an agriculturist,
and was killed by the Viet Cong.
        1. Studebaker, Ted—Juvenile literature.
2. Conscientious objectors—United States—Biography—
Juvenile literature.   3. Pacifists—United States—
Biography—Juvenile Literature.   4. Church of the
Brethren—Biography—Juvenile literature.   5. Vietnamese
Conflict, 1961-1975—United States—Juvenile literature.
[1. Studebaker, Ted.   2. Pacifists.   3. Conscientious
objectors]   I. Guenthner, Jim, ill.   II. Title.

UB343.M66   1987   355.2'24'0924   [B]   [92]   86-19419
ISBN 0-8361-3427-3 (pbk.)

This is a story about a young man named Ted Studebaker. He grew up in a large farm family of eight children. He was the seventh child born to Stanley and Zelma Studebaker.

Ted had a happy life on his family's farm. He worked and worked until he could walk on his hands around the yard.

When Ted was eight years old, he learned how to drive a tractor. His head didn't show over the steering wheel. Excited people kept coming to his parents' house, saying a tractor was in the fields with no driver!

Horseback riding was exciting to Ted.

Ted's favorite place to cool off was the farm pond. On a tall branch of a sycamore tree, his brothers had hung a heavy rope. Ted loved to swing over the pond and jump in.

Ted raised calves, chickens, and hogs on the farm.

In the winter, Ted, with brothers, sisters, and friends, played hockey on the ice for hours at a time.

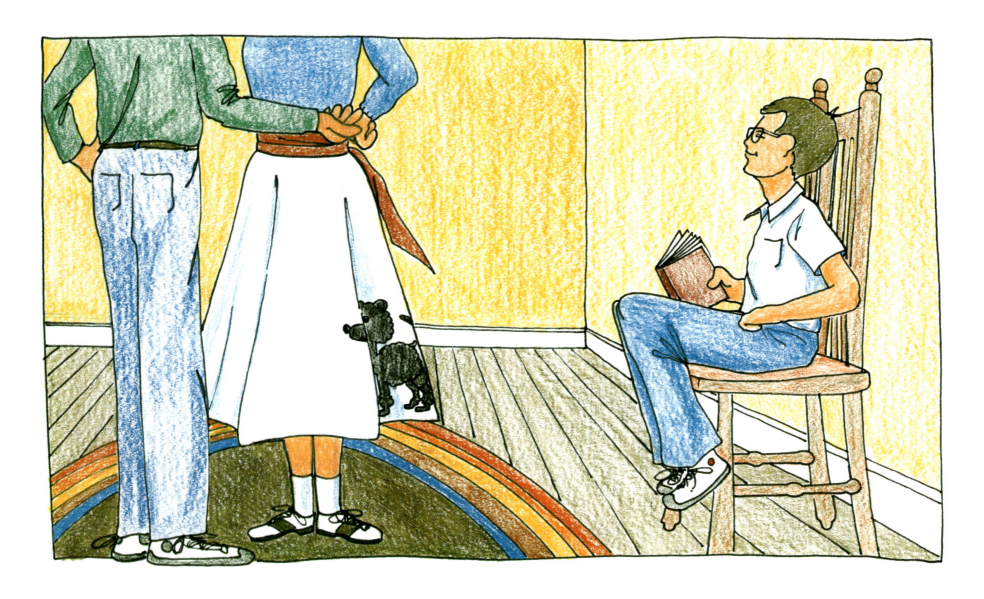

As a child, Ted was quiet and thoughtful. He paid much attention to what others had to say. He often listened and thought about ideas others had spoken, rather than talking very much.

Ted attended the West Milton Church of the Brethren. He was baptized in the family's pond into this church. He became active in the work of the church.

He enjoyed summer church camps and joined the church's youth group. The young people organized work camps to help others. Ted had a growing desire to be of service to others, especially to help people learn how to help themselves.

Ted had fun   playing his guitar. He liked to sing songs called ballads.
Music helped Ted relax.

Ted went to the Milton-Union Schools in West Milton, Ohio. Sports were an important part of Ted's life. He earned varsity awards in football . . .

and in track . . .

and in wrestling during his high school years. He also did well in these sports in college.

Ted loved these activities because they helped him learn the real meaning of being a good sport and working as a part of a team.

Ted loved to tease his younger brother, Doug. He liked to dress Doug in a football uniform when he was small.

Ted enjoyed riding a motor scooter.

Ted was interested in farming or agriculture. He studied agriculture for three years in high school and was a member of Future Farmers of America. During the summer months he worked for a plumbing and heating company to help pay for his college education.

Before Ted graduated from high school, his classmates voted him the senior male who had achieved the most during the past four years. He was given a trophy when he received this honor.

The Church of the Brethren helped Ted understand that all persons' lives are precious. Ted knew that Jesus loves all the people in the world. Ted could never kill anyone, even during war. A person with this belief is called a Christian pacifist.

Ted wrote a letter to the United States government explaining why he could not fight
and kill other people. The government said they would not force Ted to be a soldier.
They listed him as a conscientious objector (a C.O.).

Ted went to Manchester College in North Manchester, Indiana. By attending school during the summers, he finished college in three years rather than the usual four.

People were important to Ted during college. He had deep friendships with students and professors.

At Manchester, he lived in a private home with other students. He roomed with persons from Turkey, Kenya, and Burma, as well as with Americans. Though Ted was very different from some of them, he learned that they could all be friends and care about each other.

Ted studied psychology and sociology in college. Both subjects would help him serve other people with special needs. After he graduated from Manchester, Ted attended Florida State and received his master's degree in social work. Now he was ready to spend full time helping people wherever he felt God had work for him to do.

Ted had a great desire to travel around the world to fulfill his dream. Many college-age young men and women were in the Army, the Air Force, the Navy, or the Marines. But Ted wanted to serve his country for two years in a way that would help others rather than hurt or kill them.

When Ted was twenty-three, he offered to go to Vietnam and help the people there become better farmers. Ted worked for Brethren Volunteer Services with an organization called Vietnam Christian Service.

Ted lived with the people in Vietnam for two years. He helped them plant a kind of rice that could be grown more easily in higher lands. He taught them how to irrigate or water the rice. A war was going on, but Ted was not a soldier. A popular song about Ted quotes him as saying, "Give me a shovel instead of a gun. I want to help people here."

30

Ted raised chickens in a bathtub and grew vegetables and shared these with the mountain people.

Ted helped the farmers grow better crops. He set up a rice polisher, a machine that keeps the inner bran and takes off the rest, instead of doing it by hand.

In 1971 he married Ven Pak, a Chinese woman. She was a volunteer from Asian Christian Service. Ted and his new wife were happy together. But the war was still going on.

Ted knew that many people had been killed in the war in the Di Linh area where he worked. Even though Ted was not an American soldier, he knew that he was in danger. But he wanted to keep helping the Vietnamese people. He went about his work as usual. A week after the wedding, Ted was shot to death.

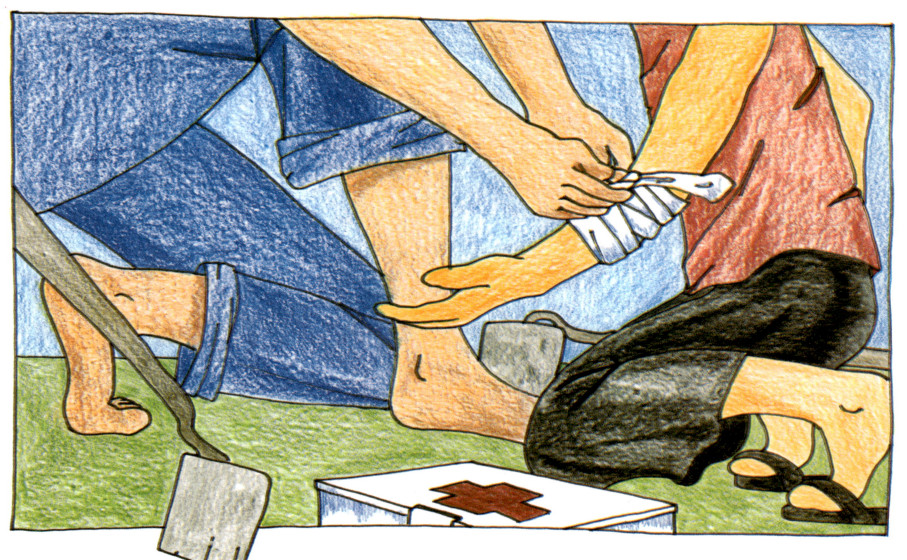

Although his family and friends were sad when Ted died, they knew that he did what God wanted him to do. He gave his life helping people rather than fighting them as a soldier. Ted has been remembered in books and records. A song has been written about him. As long as people keep the memory of Ted Studebaker in their hearts, his cruel death will serve a good purpose.

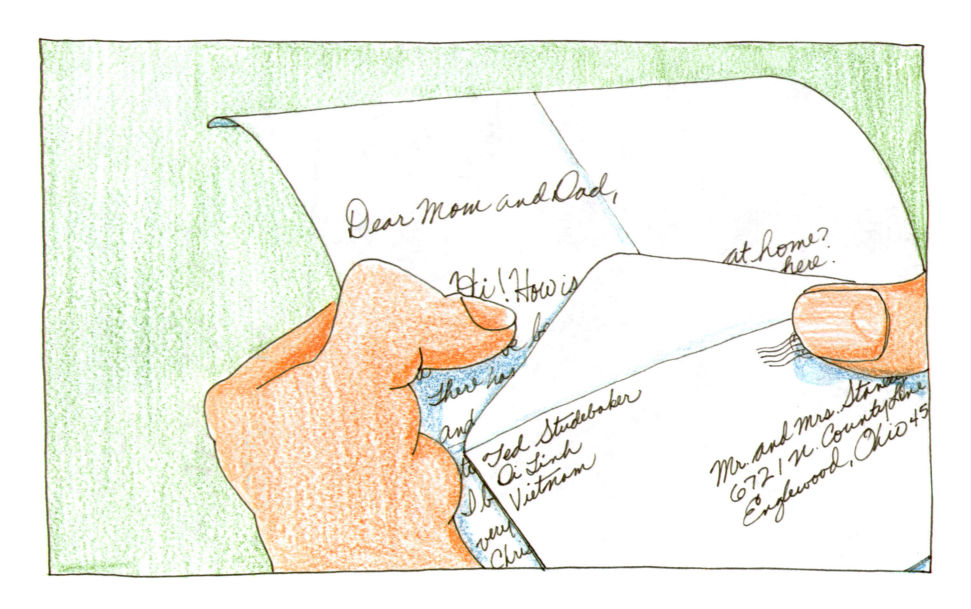

Before Ted died, he wrote a letter to his family and friends in Ohio. He explained that he was trying hard to follow the example of Jesus. "Above all, Christ taught me how to love all people, including enemies, and to return good for evil," Ted wrote.